Journey to Freedom

MADAM C. J. WALKER

BY LORI HOBKIRK

"THERE IS NO ROYAL FLOWER-STREWN PATH TO SUCCESS. AND IF THERE IS, I HAVE NOT FOUND IT, FOR IF I HAVE ACCOMPLISHED ANYTHING IN LIFE IT IS BECAUSE I HAVE BEEN WILLING TO WORK HARD."

— MADAM C. J. WALKER

Cover and page 4 caption:
Madam C. J. Walker
around 1912

Content Consultant:
A'Lelia Bundles, great-great-
granddaughter of Madam C. J.
Walker; author, On Her Own
Ground: The Life and Times
of Madam C. J. Walker

Published in the United States of America by The Child's World®
1980 Lookout Drive, Mankato, MN 56003-1705
800-599-READ • www.childsworld.com

ACKNOWLEDGEMENTS

The Child's World®: Mary Berendes, Publishing Director

The Design Lab: Kathleen Petelinsek, Design; Gregory Lindholm, Page Production

Red Line Editorial: Holly Saari, Editorial Direction

PHOTOS

Cover and page 4: A'Lelia Bundles/Walker Family Collection/www.madamcjwalker.com

Interior: A'Lelia Bundles/Walker Family Collection/www.madamcjwalker.com: 5, 6, 10, 12, 13, 15, 16, 17, 20, 21, 22, 23, 25, 26, 27; Bettmann/Corbis: 7; AP Images: 8; Corbis: 11

LIBRARY OF CONGRESS CATALOGING-IN-PUBLICATION DATA

Hobkirk, Lori.
  Madam C. J. Walker / by Lori Hobkirk.
    p. cm. — (Journey to freedom)
  Includes bibliographical references and index.
  ISBN 978-1-60253-127-7 (library bound : alk. paper)
  1. Walker, C. J., Madam, 1867–1919—Juvenile literature. 2. African American women executives—Biography—Juvenile literature. 3. Cosmetics industry—United States—History—Juvenile literature. 4. Women millionaires—United States—Biography—Juvenile literature. 5. African Americans—Biography. 6. Cosmetics industry—History. I. Title. II. Series.

HD9970.5.C672W3544 2009
338.7'66855092—dc22
[B]

2008031933

CONTENTS

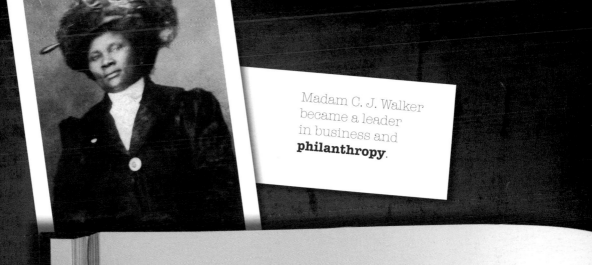

Madam C. J. Walker
became a leader
in business and
philanthropy.

Chapter One

PAVING THE WAY

tarting a business and making it successful is not an easy task. It was even more difficult for a black woman to accomplish this in the 1900s. Yet, this is what Madam C. J. Walker did.

Originally named Sarah Breedlove, Madam C. J. Walker was born in 1867. Slavery had ended only two years earlier. Her family was free, but life in the South was still difficult. **Discrimination** and **prejudice** against black people still existed. Her family had little money. She worked hard when she was young to help her family in any way that she could. Hard work played an important role throughout Walker's life. It is one reason why she achieved so much.

After she grew up and moved to the northern United States, Walker developed a line of hair-care products specifically for black women. She worked hard to advertise and sell them. Through these products, she became well known as Madam C. J. Walker and became quite wealthy.

With her success and wealth, Walker helped others. She realized one of the most important things in her life was to help other black women. She did this in two ways. She provided excellent hair-care products for these women to use in order to improve themselves. And she helped them find work through her company.

Madam C. J. Walker proved women could become independent and successful. Her hard work and business savvy paved the way for other women to become successful in business. She also showed that it was important to give back to others.

Madam C. J. Walker, along with Booker T. Washington (with hat in hand) at the dedication of a YMCA in Indianapolis, Indiana

Chapter Two

UP THE MISSISSIPPI

arah Breedlove was born on December 23, 1867. She was the fifth of six children, and the first person in her family not born into slavery. It was the beginning of a new era. The U.S. Civil War had ended two years earlier. Slaves were finally free.

The Breedloves lived in the small village of Delta, Louisiana, on the banks of the Mississippi River. After the war, they worked as **sharecroppers** on one of the smaller cotton plantations in the area.

Although slaves were now free, life was still very difficult for black people. Sarah, her sister, and her four brothers worked all day in the cotton fields with their parents. The family also raised chickens and sold eggs. The children had no shoes to wear.

It was common for former slaves to work on plantations as sharecroppers.

Each night, Sarah helped her mother and sister with the housework. They did laundry for other families to earn extra money.

The Breedloves lived in this cabin (often in unsanitary conditions) in Delta, Louisiana.

Like many black children in the South at the time, the Breedlove children could not go to school. They were too busy working. The Breedlove children probably would not have attended school even if they had the time. Blacks and whites could not attend the same schools. Very few schools for black children existed because there was no government funding for them.

When Sarah was seven years old, both of her parents became ill. **Epidemics** affected former slaves especially hard. In the rural area where the Breedloves lived, living conditions were often unsanitary. The family was exhausted from working hard and seldom had enough healthful food to eat. Because they were so poor, they could not go to the best doctors, who usually treated only white people.

Sarah's mother died during a cholera epidemic. When her father died the next year, Sarah and her baby brother, Solomon, were left in the care of her sister, Louvenia. Her older brothers had moved across the river to Vicksburg,

The Mississippi River was a symbol of freedom to many former slaves in the region. They believed it could transport them to a new and better life.

After working in the cotton fields all day, Sarah was tired. She often looked across the river to the town of Vicksburg, Mississippi. She longed for the "Promised Land," a place where blacks would have the same opportunities as whites.

Mississippi, where they found jobs. Now Sarah's life had become even more difficult, as she and Louvenia had to work extra hard just to have enough food to eat.

Soon, Sarah, Louvenia, and Solomon moved to Vicksburg hoping to escape disease and poverty. However, so many poor people had fled to Vicksburg that jobs were difficult to find. Louvenia was lucky to find work as a washerwoman. She washed, ironed, and folded clothes. Sarah did whatever she could to help her.

Louvenia married a man named Jesse Powell, whom Sarah did not like. She thought Jesse was cruel and angry. Sarah longed to get away from him. She wanted the chance to go to school and to change her life. She dreamed of being the best person she could be.

Sarah took the first step toward independence at age 14 when she married a man named Moses McWilliams. Three years later, she gave birth to her only child, a daughter named Lelia. Moses died not long after. Sarah was only 20 years old. She was a widow, and she had a young daughter to support. It was a difficult time, but she refused to move back in with Louvenia and Jesse.

Sarah continued to work hard. She hoped to find a way to move to St. Louis, where her older brothers worked as barbers. She finally earned enough money to buy two tickets on a riverboat. Sarah and Lelia were bound for Missouri, traveling up the Mississippi River to a better life. Sarah was nervous to move so far away, but she also was ready for a change.

Sarah and her daughter moved to St. Louis, Missouri, to begin a new life.

Chapter Three

FOLLOWING A DREAM

In 1888, Sarah and Lelia arrived in St. Louis. The size of the city amazed them. More than 500,000 people lived in St. Louis, and it had one of the nation's largest black populations. Approximately 35,000 black people lived in the city. Like Sarah, many southern black people moved to St. Louis hoping to find a better life. Workers earned more money in St. Louis than in the South, where most jobs were on farms. In the city, black people worked as servants, cooks, and laborers. A few became teachers, ministers, and doctors.

One of Sarah's main reasons for moving to St. Louis was to give her daughter a better life.

In St. Louis, three newspapers were published specifically for black readers. Black people also owned more than 100 businesses in the city.

Walker's daughter, Lelia, in 1923

Living in St. Louis allowed Sarah and Lelia to be closer to Sarah's brothers. It also allowed her to become involved in the community and form new friendships.

Upon arriving in St. Louis, Sarah joined St. Paul African Methodist Episcopal Church. The church was well known in the black community. Its members helped each other in many ways. The church members helped Sarah find work in her new city.

Sarah now had two goals: to provide a good life for herself and her daughter and to get an education for both of them. These seemed like simple wishes. But discrimination against blacks existed in the North as well. Employers paid black workers far less than they paid white workers. In order to make enough money to make ends meet, Sarah worked long hours six days a week doing laundry. She worked at home so she could care for Lelia at the same time.

Once Sarah was settled, she wanted to help other women like herself. She was grateful for the church's generosity. She wanted to do something in return. She joined the church's Mite Missionary Society, which helped poor people in need. Sarah offered a helping hand whenever she could and continued to do so for the rest of her life.

Lelia grew up during Sarah's years of hard work. Sarah saved money whenever she could. She planned to send Lelia to college. At the time, very few girls went to college. It was almost unheard of for a young, black woman to do so. However, Sarah refused to think it could not be done. When the time came, Lelia moved to Tennessee to attend Knoxville College, a school for black students.

Sarah's effort and sacrifice throughout her life did have their price. For one thing, she did not have much time to care for her appearance. She had been losing her hair for many years due to a scalp disease caused by severe dandruff and poor health habits. During this time, many people did not have indoor bathrooms or electricity. Taking a bath and washing one's hair were not a part of daily **hygiene** practices. As a result, Sarah and many other women were losing their hair.

Like many women, Sarah wanted her hair to look beautiful, but she could not find products that were made for her naturally curly hair. The liquid tonics that were made for white women, who usually had naturally straight hair, made her hair drier and more brittle. Sometimes the harsh chemicals burned her scalp and caused more hair loss.

Sarah and other black women struggled to find hair products that would work for their hair type. Sarah continued to use **ointments** that she thought would soften her hair and make it easier to comb and style.

Before the civil war, Missouri had been a **slave state**. At the time, Sarah's church had run a secret school to teach blacks to read and write. After the war, church members helped former slaves find work, housing, clothing, and food.

Sarah told the story of her dream whenever people asked how she discovered the hair-growth recipe. For most of her life, the exact recipe was shared with only two other people: her daughter, Lelia, and her friend and coworker, Alice Kelly.

One night, Sarah tried to mix her own hair-growth ointment. She hoped she could discover the correct ingredients. In that night of restless sleep, a black man came to Sarah in a dream. He whispered the names of special ingredients. He said they would help make her hair grow. The next morning, Sarah prepared her new ointment. Soon, she would be selling it to black women all across the United States.

The real secret to Sarah's system of hair care was the combination of a vegetable-based shampoo and an ointment that contained sulfur. She urged her customers to wash their hair more often. Once their scalps were clean, Sarah carefully rubbed in the ointment at the roots. Soon the sulfur, which healed sores and dandruff, cured their scalp infections.

At the age of 37, Sarah moved to Denver, Colorado, to join her sister-in-law, Lucy, the widow of one of Sarah's brothers. It was the beginning of a new life. Her hair was growing back. She began to make plans to sell her ointment to other women.

BEFORE USING

Sarah's first newspaper advertisement showed photos of her hair before and after using her hair-care products.

The Vegetable Shampoo became a popular product among Sarah's customers.

Chapter Four

ON THE ROAD

arah liked Denver very much. Its bright blue skies were so different from the heavy, muggy air of St. Louis. Not as many black people lived there, but the black community was growing. People's attitudes were also different. It was a place of **expansion** and new ideas.

In the late 1800s, many Denver residents had struck gold in the Rocky Mountains. They used their wealth to build large houses and businesses. A few black people also had started businesses and prospered in the city as well. Yet discrimination against black people still occurred.

Sarah continued to work hard. She did laundry two days a week and worked as a cook for a local pharmacist named E. L. Scholtz. When Scholtz saw her experimenting with her products, he offered to analyze her formula. He helped perfect her shampoo and ointment.

Sarah enlisted the help of her sister-in-law. They tried different mixtures on their hair. Sarah wanted to make a good, **reliable** product. Within a few months, Sarah had created five hair-care products. They contained key ingredients to treat the hair and scalp in several ways. Her hair began to grow thick and long.

Once she refined her hair-care formulas, she decided to package and sell them. She visited every house in her neighborhood and talked to women in her church. She used her own hair as an example of how well the products worked. After seeing Sarah's long, healthy hair, other women would often try the products.

Sarah's most popular and bestselling product was Wonderful Hair Grower, which treated dandruff and healed scalp infections. Vegetable Shampoo cleansed the hair and Glossine made it softer. Tetter Salve and Temple Grower were stronger versions of Walker's Wonderful Hair Grower.

The packaging for Wonderful Hair Grower, around 1906

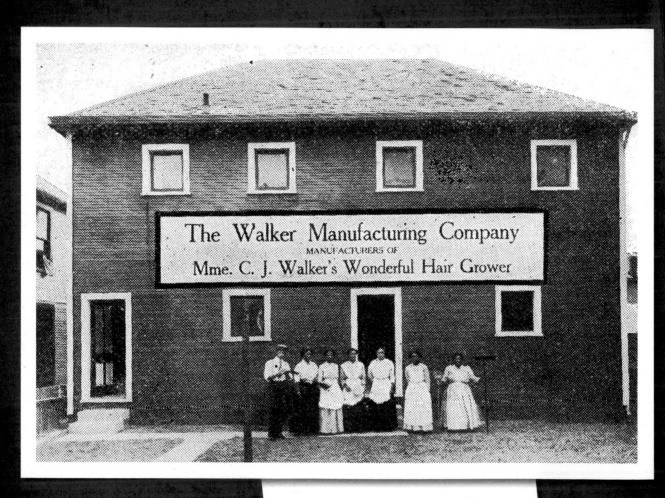

Madam C. J. Walker's company
employed workers in her factories
and agents throughout the country.

Around this time, Charles Joseph Walker, better known as C. J., came to Denver to visit Sarah. He was a friend from St. Louis. It was a happy reunion for both of them. They married in January 1906.

C. J. worked in the newspaper business. Together, they devised a plan to sell her hair-care products. Sarah began calling herself Madam C. J. Walker. It was a smart move; the title was memorable and sounded important. She kept the title for the rest of her life, even after she and C. J. divorced.

Walker knew the look of her own hair helped sell products. She also believed that she could increase sales if she dressed well. With a new name, a dark skirt, and a crisp white blouse, Walker continued to sell her products door to door. She also advertised in black newspapers across the country. A photograph showing her long hair was placed on the packages of her products.

Her business began to grow. Walker started a mail-order department so women could order and receive products through the mail. Orders came in from across the country. Lelia had recently graduated from Knoxville College. Walker asked her to help with the expanding business.

With C. J. and Lelia's help, Walker's company began to make a profit of ten dollars per week. Few women had jobs outside their homes, so most did not earn their own money. Such a salary was unheard of for a woman at the time. Walker now earned four times

At 21 years old, Lelia stood a striking six feet tall. She was also very smart. At the time, not many black women were college educated. Lelia's intelligence, dignity, and poise were great additions to her mother's business.

Sarah (front row center) with a group of Ohio agents, around 1915

what she once made doing laundry. She decided to use the company's growing profits to continue to expand the business.

Walker and her husband left Denver for a year and a half to travel across the country and sell her products. During this time, she realized another way to grow her business. If she hired some of her customers as salespeople, she could sell even more products. Walker trained other women to demonstrate the hair-care products. In exchange, the salespeople received a **commission**.

It proved to be a successful plan. Walker's company gave other black women new opportunities. They could become "hair culturists," as Walker called her salespeople, instead of cooks or servants. With her salespeople's help, Walker had more time to create new marketing plans and interesting advertisements. The company continued to grow, and profits increased to $35 per week. This was more than many white businesses made at the time.

In 1908, Walker and her husband, C. J., decided to move to the eastern United States. They chose Pittsburgh, Pennsylvania, as their new home. The Northeast had a larger population of black residents than Colorado and the western United States. From Pittsburgh they could travel easily to other large cities on the East Coast. Also, steel was manufactured in Pittsburgh. That was important for manufacturing another of Walker's products: the steel comb. Walker's hair-care business blossomed in the new city. She opened a school, which she named after her daughter. At Lelia College, women were trained in the "Walker Method" of sales and in "hair culture."

Walker settled in Pittsburgh for only a year and a half. She was not content to slow down now that her company was successful. She wanted to make sure all black women heard about her products. She searched for another city with a large black population. After many trips throughout the United States, Walker moved to Indianapolis, Indiana, in 1910. Indianapolis was located on a busy train route that connected cities from all across the United States. It was a good place to build a factory and to distribute her line of products.

Lelia—who had changed her name to A'Lelia— stayed in Pittsburgh. She ran Lelia College while Walker continued to build the business in Indianapolis. After one year in that city, Walker's company employed nearly 1,000 "Walker agents" across the country. Her factory employed approximately two dozen neighborhood people. Walker also employed women in some of the company's most important positions, including factory manager.

Tuition *at Lelia College cost $25. Walker offered* **scholarships** *to those who could not afford it. Women came from all over the country for instruction. Others learned her hair-care methods through* **correspondence courses**

Many Walker hair culturists opened their own salons.

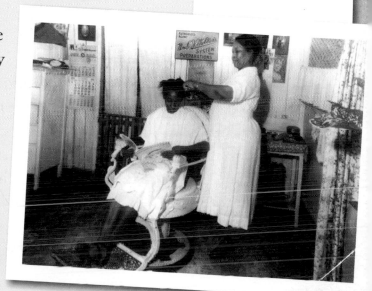

Madam C. J. Walker (driver's seat) learned how to drive and owned several cars.

Chapter Five

SHARING THE WEALTH

In six years, Madam C. J. Walker had gone from selling her products door-to-door in Denver to employing 4,000 people nationwide. Her agents did more than just sell hair-care supplies. With Walker's guidance, they also became involved in business and their communities. Many opened their own Walker beauty parlors in cities around the country.

Walker's business was running well and earning an excellent profit, but Walker was not about to retire. She continued to build her company and increase her sales. She realized her dream of learning to read and write. She not only learned how to drive, she owned several cars at a time when very few women knew how to drive. She traveled throughout the United States, Central America, and the Caribbean. She became knowledgeable about literature, theater, and current events.

Money was not the most important thing in Walker's life. She had always felt the need to help people, and now she could use her business to do it. She was proud of what she had accomplished. Teaching black women to tend more to their appearance gave them confidence. Perhaps most important, Walker helped many black people fulfill their own dreams of success and independence. Her company provided jobs for thousands of people.

In Indianapolis, Walker hired black workers for her factory. She had housing built for black residents of Indianapolis. She hired black construction workers because she knew white companies would not hire them. It was important to Walker to treat her employees with dignity and respect.

The graduating class of 1939 from a Walker beauty school in St. Louis, Missouri

Walker shared the money she earned. She donated to the Young Men's Christian Association (YMCA). She gave money to the National Association of Colored Women (NACW). She also donated money to schools dedicated to educating black students, such as the Tuskegee Institute and Bethune-Cookman College. She gave $5,000 to the National Association for the Advancement of Colored People (NAACP), which worked toward black equality. It was the largest donation the organization had ever received.

Throughout her life, Walker continued to support the NAACP and other organizations. It pleased her to know that she could have a positive influence on the lives of others. Walker wanted people to associate her company with generosity and goodness. Women who worked for Walker were given awards for their good deeds. In 1916, she created the National Beauty Culturists and Benevolent Association of Madam C. J. Walker Agents. Each member paid 25 cents a month to a special fund. If any member became sick or died, $50 was sent to that woman's family.

Of course, Walker did enjoy some of the money she worked hard to earn. In 1916, she began building the home of her dreams in Irvington-on-Hudson, New York. Walker named the mansion Villa Lewaro by using the first two letters of her daughter's names, A'Lelia Walker Robinson—Le-Wa-Ro. When Walker died on May 25, 1919, she left the house to A'Lelia. In 1976,

The first National Convention of Walker Agents in 1917. Walker is in the front row to the right of the man in the suit.

Villa Lewaro was listed on the National Register of Historic Places. Today it is a private residence.

Shortly before her death, Walker summoned her lawyer. With his help, she created a list of black charities and institutions to which she donated a total of $25,000. She still highly valued education and made many gifts to schools for black students.

Walker died at the age of 51. After her death, Walker's attorney, factory manager, and other Walker agents ran the company. Many of Walker's loyal employees continued to work for the company. It remained in business until 1985, when the owners sold its product rights.

Walker only lived at Villa Lewaro for one year before she died. During that time, it was the center of many important events. Talented authors and artists came to Villa Lewaro for gatherings.

Villa Lewaro hosted many gatherings, including the National Convention of Walker Agents in 1924.

Walker created a large, successful company. In 1918, she became the country's first black, female millionaire. When she died one year later, more than 25,000 women were selling her products as commissioned sales agents. Her company was earning $500,000 a year.

Madam C. J. Walker believed that people are never truly successful unless they find a way to share their success. She taught other black women how to feel good about themselves. She provided opportunities for them to improve not only their appearances but their lives as well.

In 1998, Madam C. J. Walker became the twenty-first person to be honored on a postage stamp in the Black Heritage series.

TIME LINE

1860   1870   1880

1867
Sarah Breedlove is born on December 23 in Delta, Louisiana.

1874
Sarah's parents die within a few months of each other.

1878
Sarah, her sister, Louvenia, and her brother Solomon move to Vicksburg, Mississippi.

1882
Sarah marries Moses McWilliams.

1885
Sarah and Moses have a daughter, Lelia.

1887
Moses McWilliams dies.

1888
Sarah and Lelia arrive in St. Louis, Missouri.

1904
Sarah begins experimenting with hair-care products.

1905
Sarah moves to Denver, Colorado, and finalizes her Wonderful Hair Grower and Vegetable Shampoo.

1906
Sarah Breedlove McWilliams marries Charles Joseph "C. J." Walker. She changes her name to Madam C. J. Walker.

1908
Walker moves to Pittsburgh, Pennsylvania, and opens Lelia College.

1910
Walker moves to Indianapolis, Indiana, where a company factory is built.

1912
Walker continues traveling around the country, selling products to black women.

1913
Walker's daughter, A'Lelia, moves to Harlem in New York City. She opens a second Lelia College and beauty salon.

1916
Walker builds her mansion, Villa Lewaro, in Irvington-on-Hudson, New York. Walker begins the National Beauty Culturists and Benevolent Association of Madam C. J. Walker Agents.

1917
Walker hosts her first national convention of Walker sales agents and beauty culturists in Philadelphia.

1919
Walker dies on May 25 at the age of 51.

GLOSSARY

commission
(kuh-**mish**-uhn)
Money paid to an employee for making a sale is called a commission. Walker's salespeople received commissions.

correspondence courses
(kor-uh-**spon**-duhns **kors**-ez)
Classes taken through the mail are correspondence courses. Some Walker agents took correspondence courses.

discrimination
(diss-krim-i-**nay**-shun)
Discrimination is unfair treatment of people based on differences of race, gender, religion, or culture. Growing up, Walker and her family experienced discrimination because they were black.

epidemics
(ep-uh-**dem**-iks)
Epidemics are diseases that spread rapidly through a group of people. An epidemic of cholera killed Walker's mother.

expansion
(ek-**span**-shun)
An expansion is the increase in the size of something. When Walker arrived in Denver, the city was in a period of expansion.

hygiene
(**hye**-jeen)
Hygiene is the action taken to keep oneself healthy and clean. Before Walker invented her hair-care products, she did not have good hair hygiene practices.

ointments
(**oynt**-muhnts)
Thick salves used for healing are called ointments. Walker invented ointments that improved the condition of black women's scalps.

philanthropy
(fuh-**lan**-thruh-pee)
Giving time or money to causes or charities is philanthropy. Walker used some of her profits for philanthropy.

prejudice
(**prej**-uh-diss)
Prejudice is a negative feeling or opinion about someone without just cause. White people often felt prejudice against black people because of their race.

reliable
(re-**lye**-uh-buhl)
If something is reliable, it is trustworthy. Walker wanted her products to be reliable.

scholarships
(**skahl**-ur-ships)
Sums of money awarded to students to help pay for their education are called scholarships. Walker offered scholarships to women who wanted to attend Lelia College.

sharecroppers
(**shayr**-krop-perz)
Sharecroppers are farmers who work on another person's land and receive part of the crop, or a portion of the crop sales, as payment. Walker's family worked as sharecroppers when she was growing up.

slave state
(**slayv** state)
A slave state was a U.S. state where slavery was legal. Missouri was a slave state before the U.S. Civil War.

tuition
(too-**ish**-uhn)
Tuition is a fee for attending school. Tuition at Lelia College cost $25.

FURTHER INFORMATION

Books

Bundles, A'Lelia. *On Her Own Ground: The Life and Times of Madam C. J. Walker*. New York: Scribner, 2002.

Hudson, Wade. *Scientists, Healers, and Inventors*. East Orange, NJ: Just Us Books, 2002.

Lobb, Nancy. *16 Extraordinary American Entrepreneurs*. Portland, ME: Walch Publishing, 2007.

McPherson, James M. *Into the West: From Reconstruction to the Final Days of the American Frontier*. New York: Simon & Schuster, 2006.

Sullivan, Otha Richard, and James Haskins, ed. *Black Stars: African American Women Scientists and Inventors*. New York: Wiley, 2001.

Worth, Richard, and Philip Schwarz, ed. *African Americans During Reconstruction*. New York: Chelsea House, 2006.

Videos

African American Lives. Dir. Graham Judd. PBS Paramount, 2006.

Black History: Contributions to Society in the Arts, Sports, Science, and More. St. Clair Vision, 2007.

Web Sites

Visit our Web page for links about Madam C. J. Walker:

http://www.childsworld.com/links

NOTE TO PARENTS, TEACHERS, AND LIBRARIANS: We routinely verify our Web links to make sure they are safe, active sites—so encourage your readers to check them out!

INDEX